Spanish Swear Word Coloring Book

By: Shazza T. Jones

I0465357

Introduction

Learn some Spanish swear words while you sit back and color the pages.

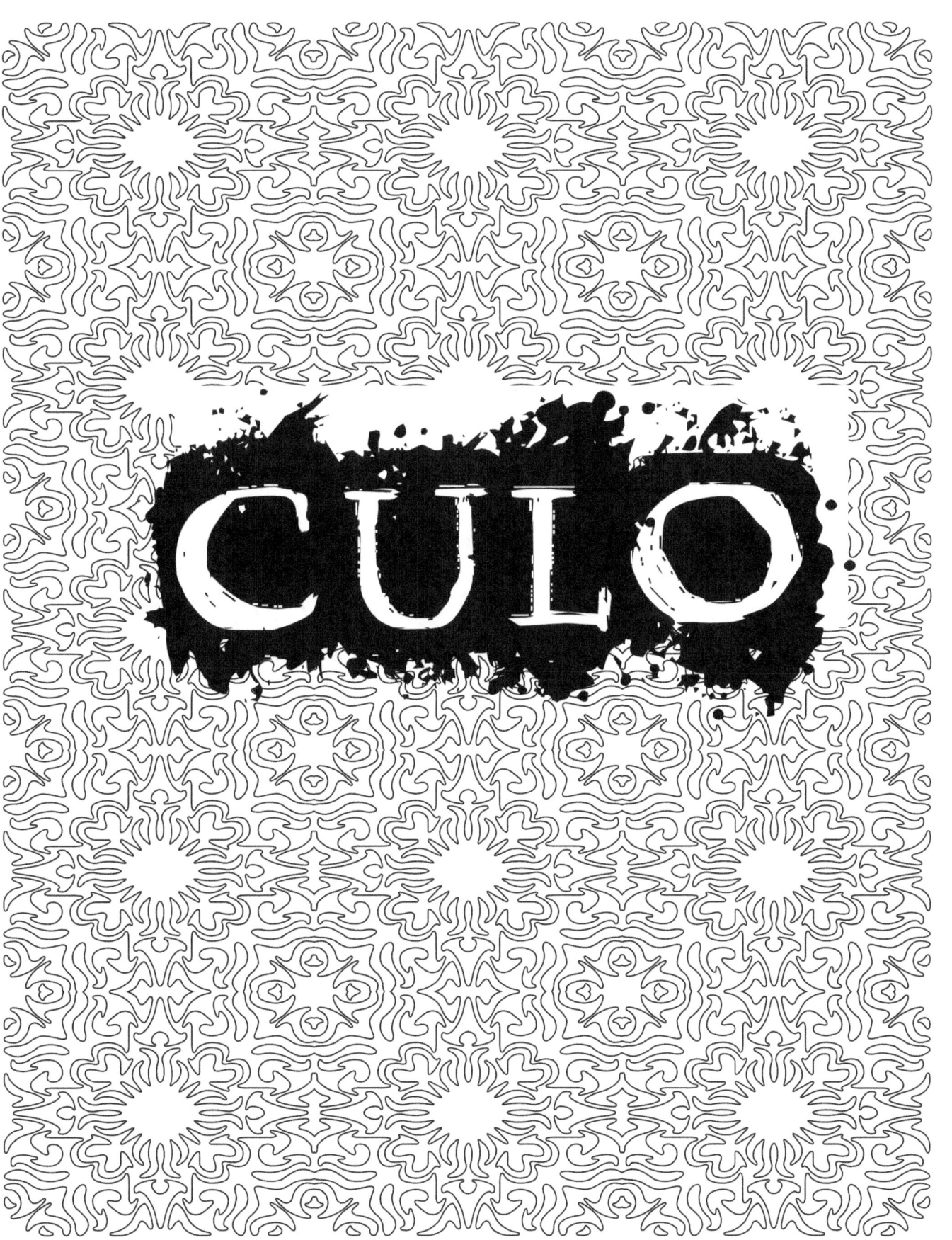

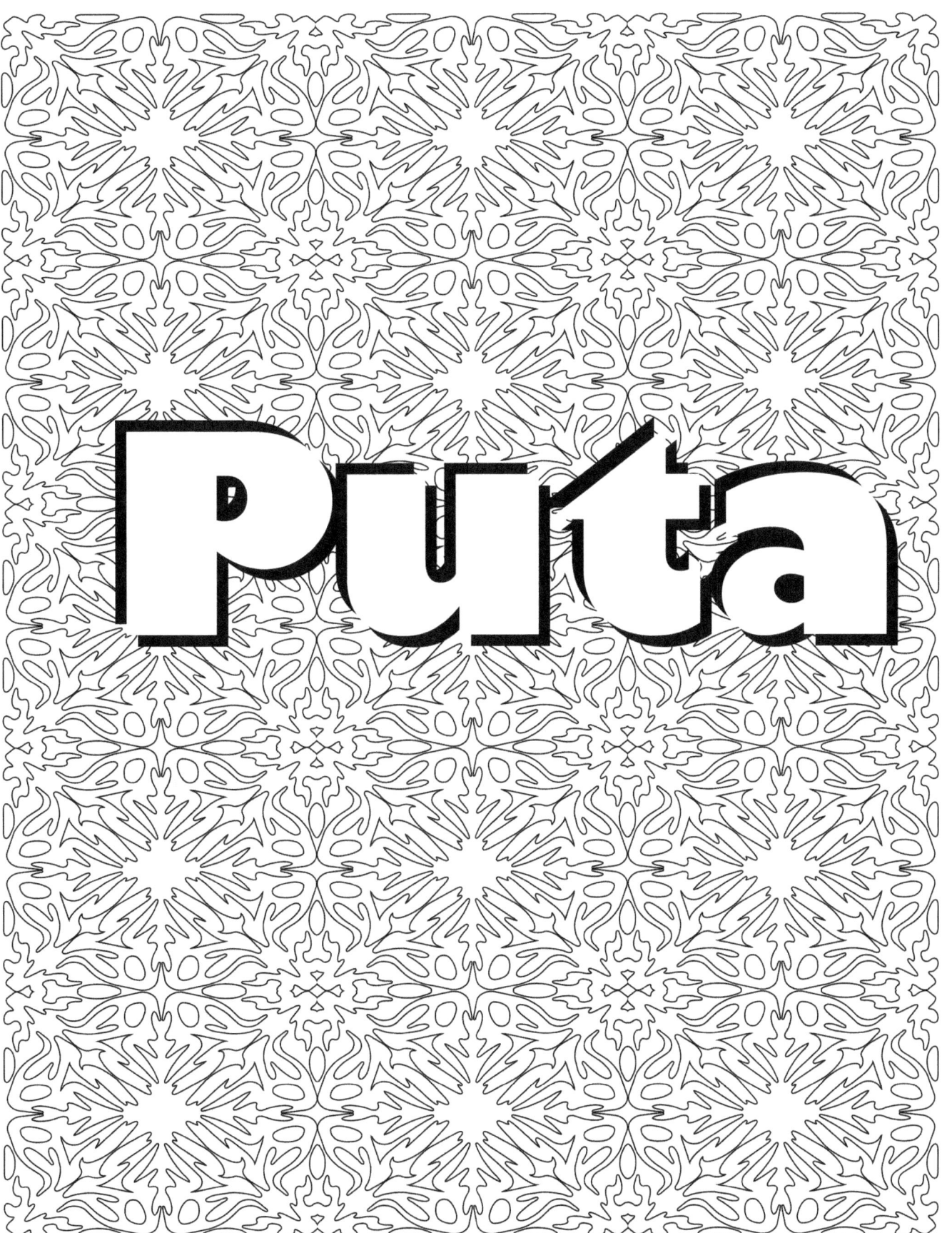

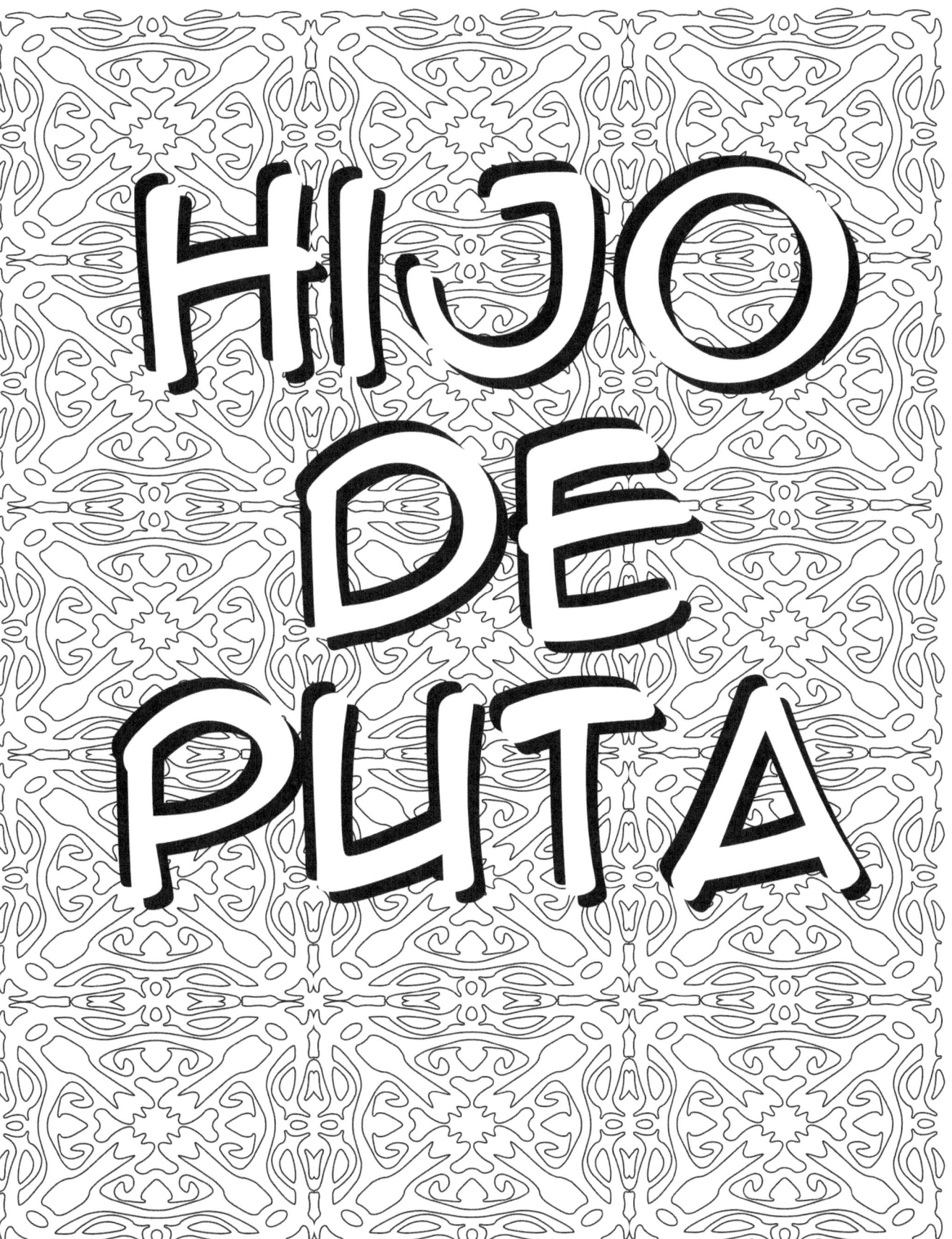

PENDEJO

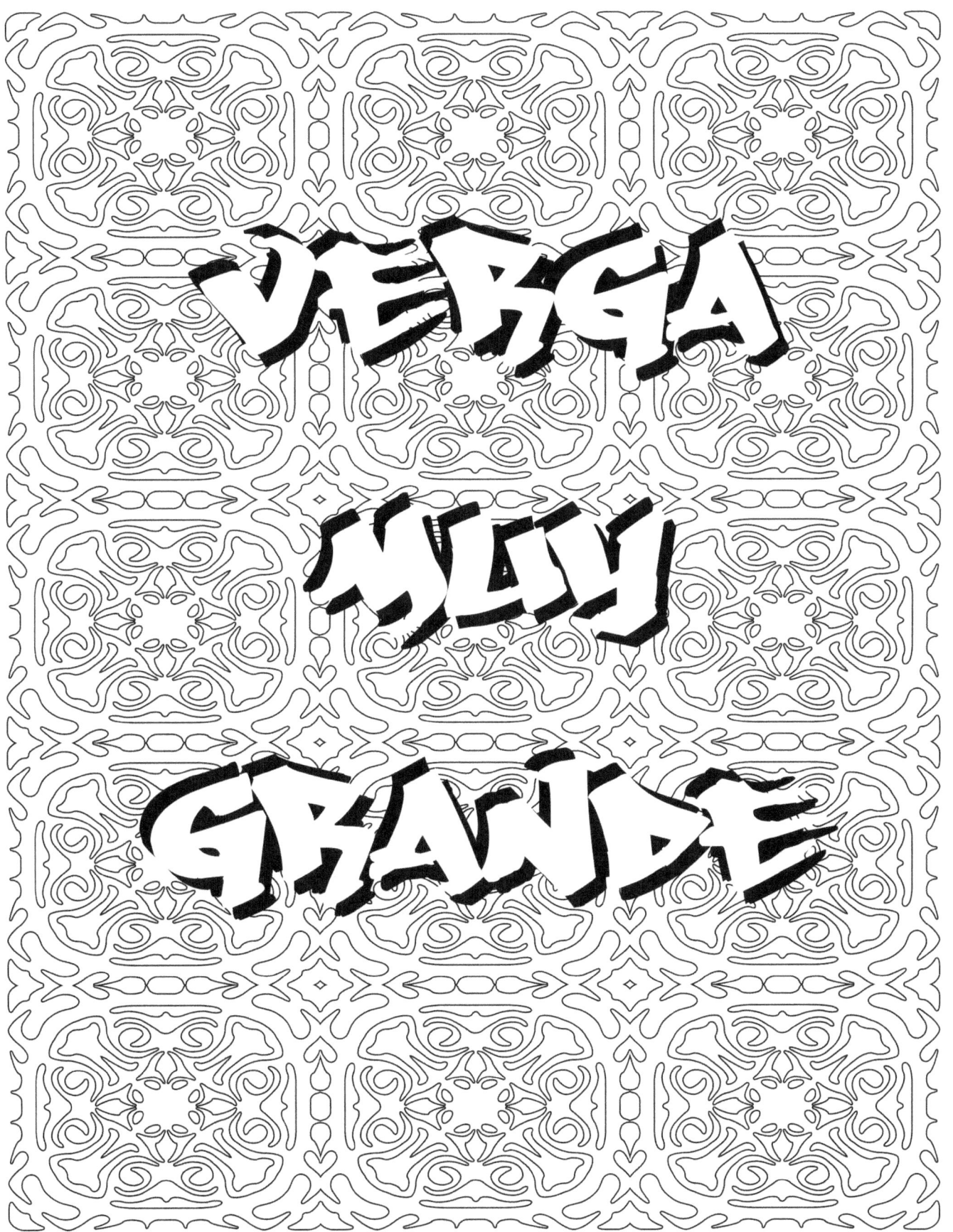

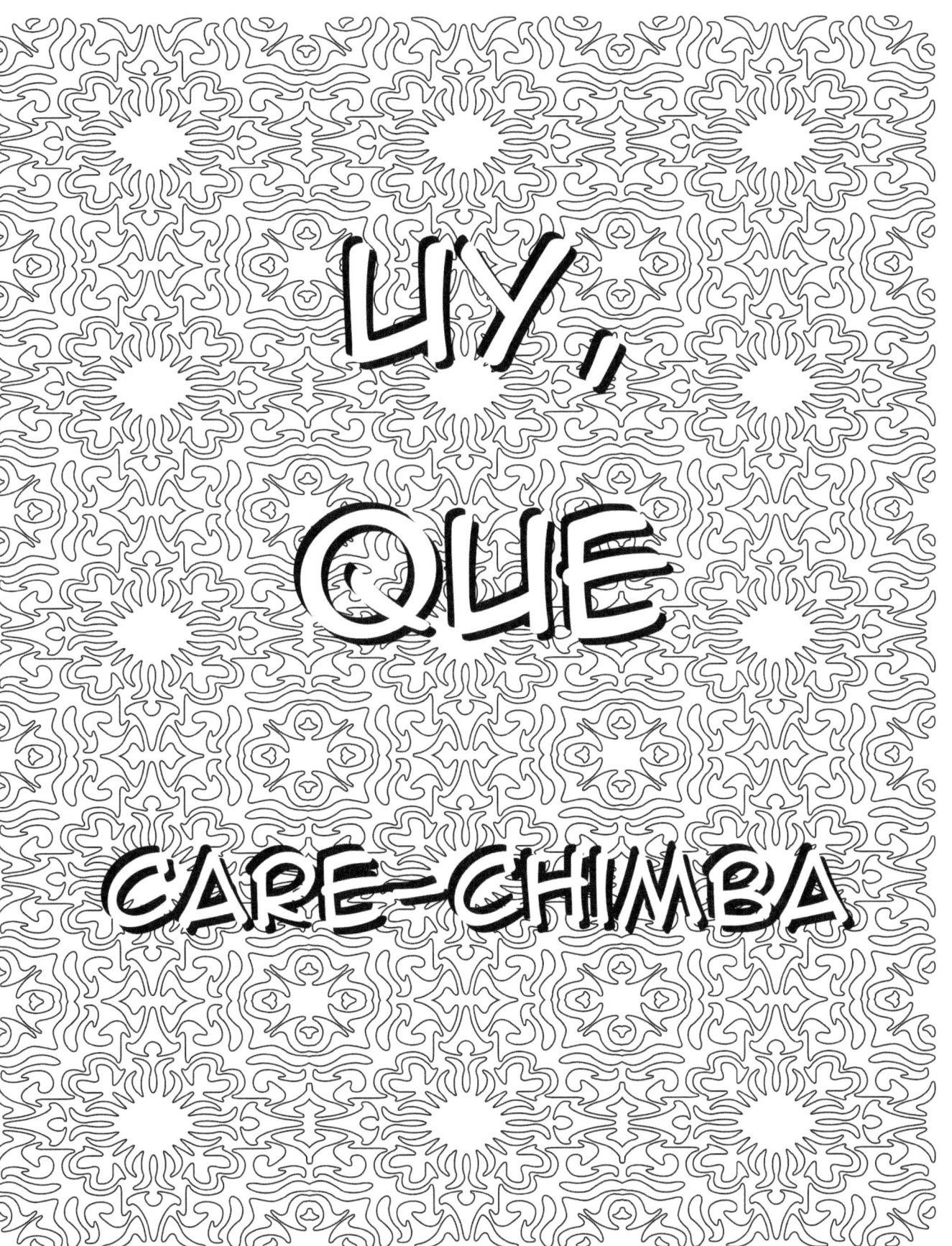

QUE TE JODAN

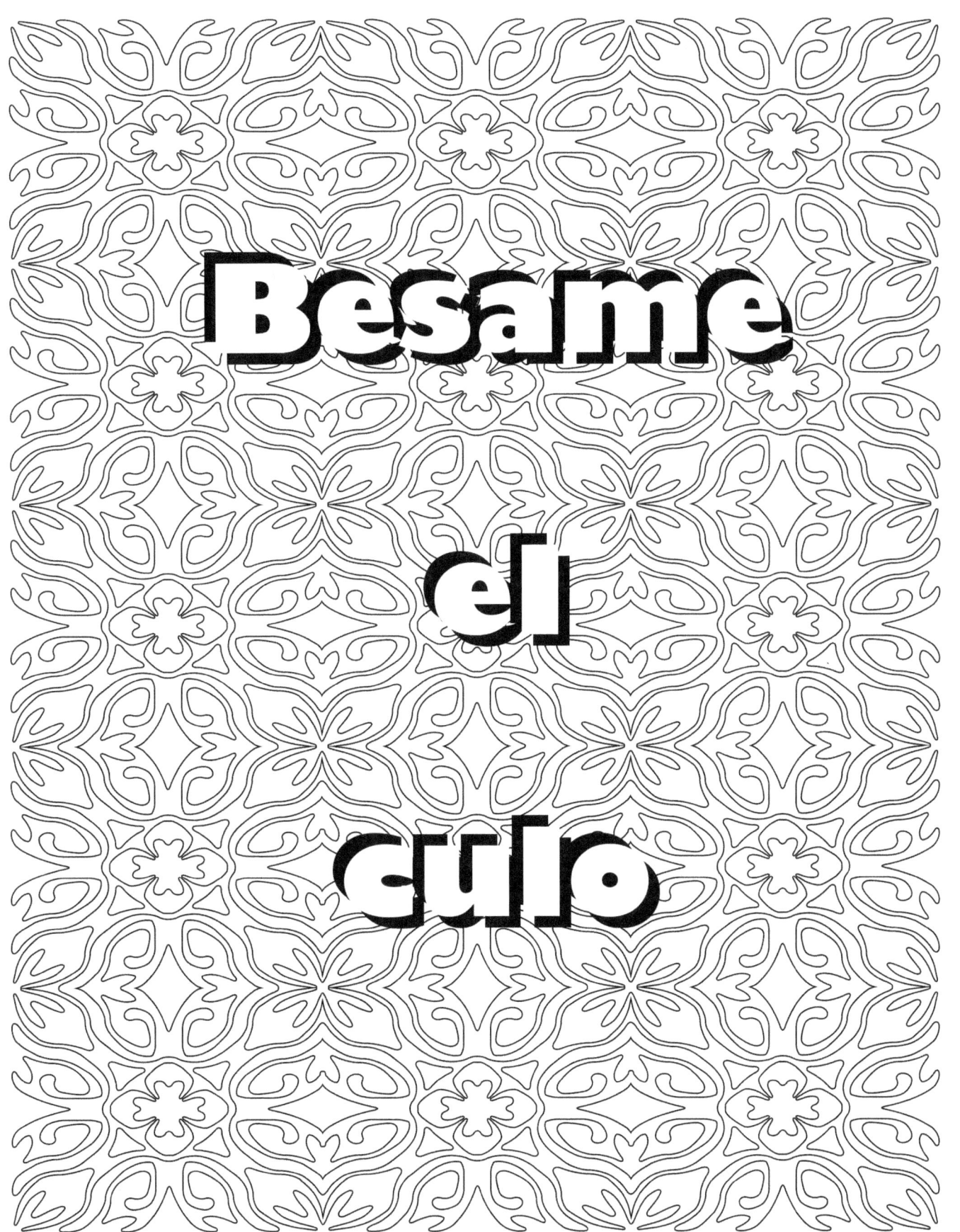

HUELES

A

MIERDA

TU MADRE ES UNA
PUTA FEA

Tengo ganas

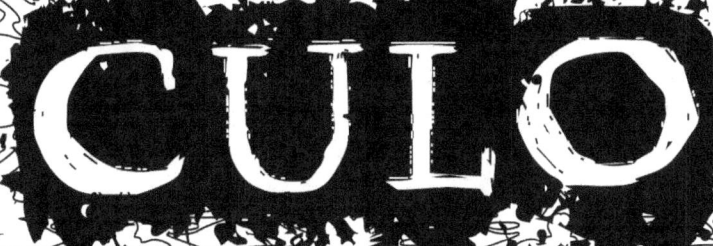

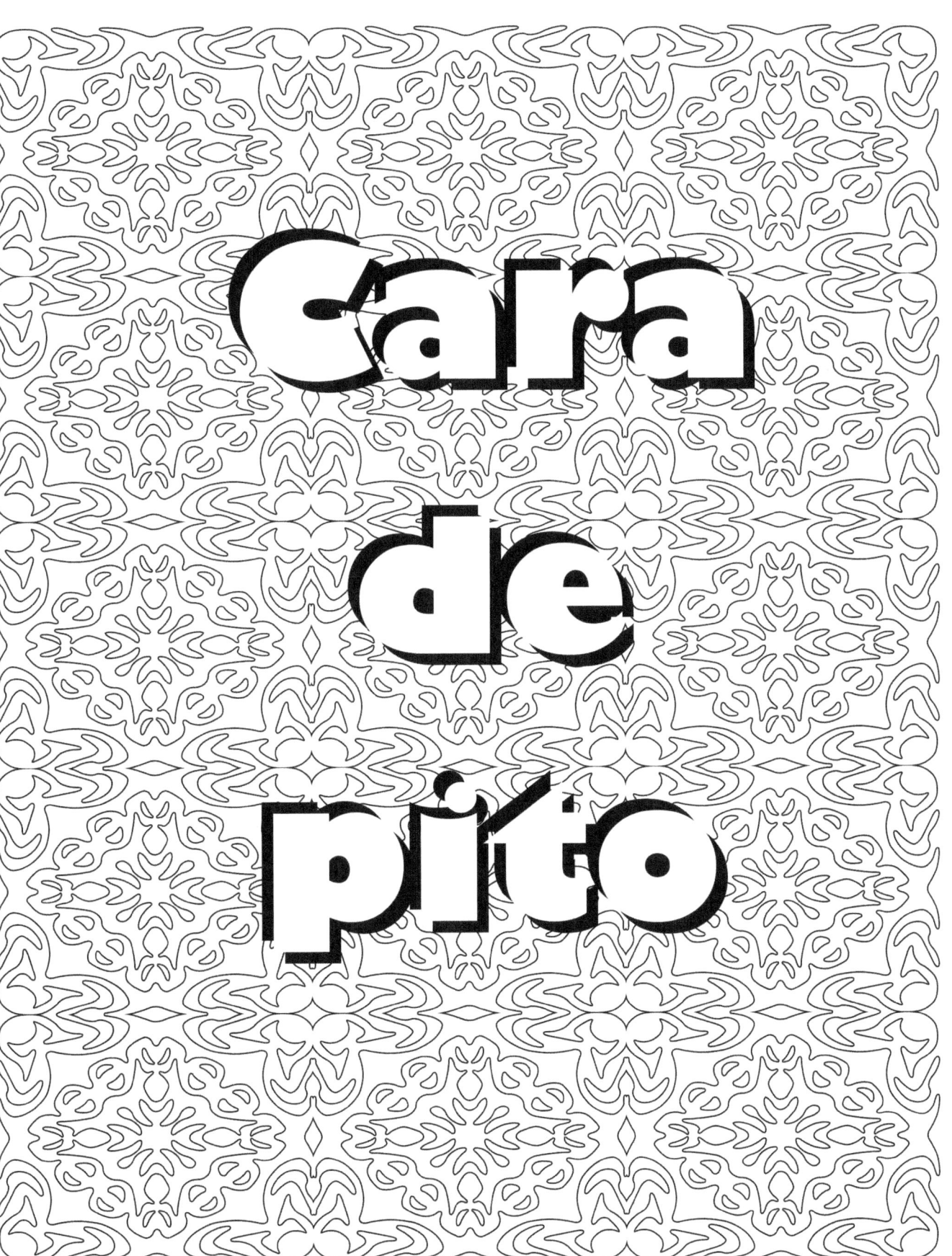

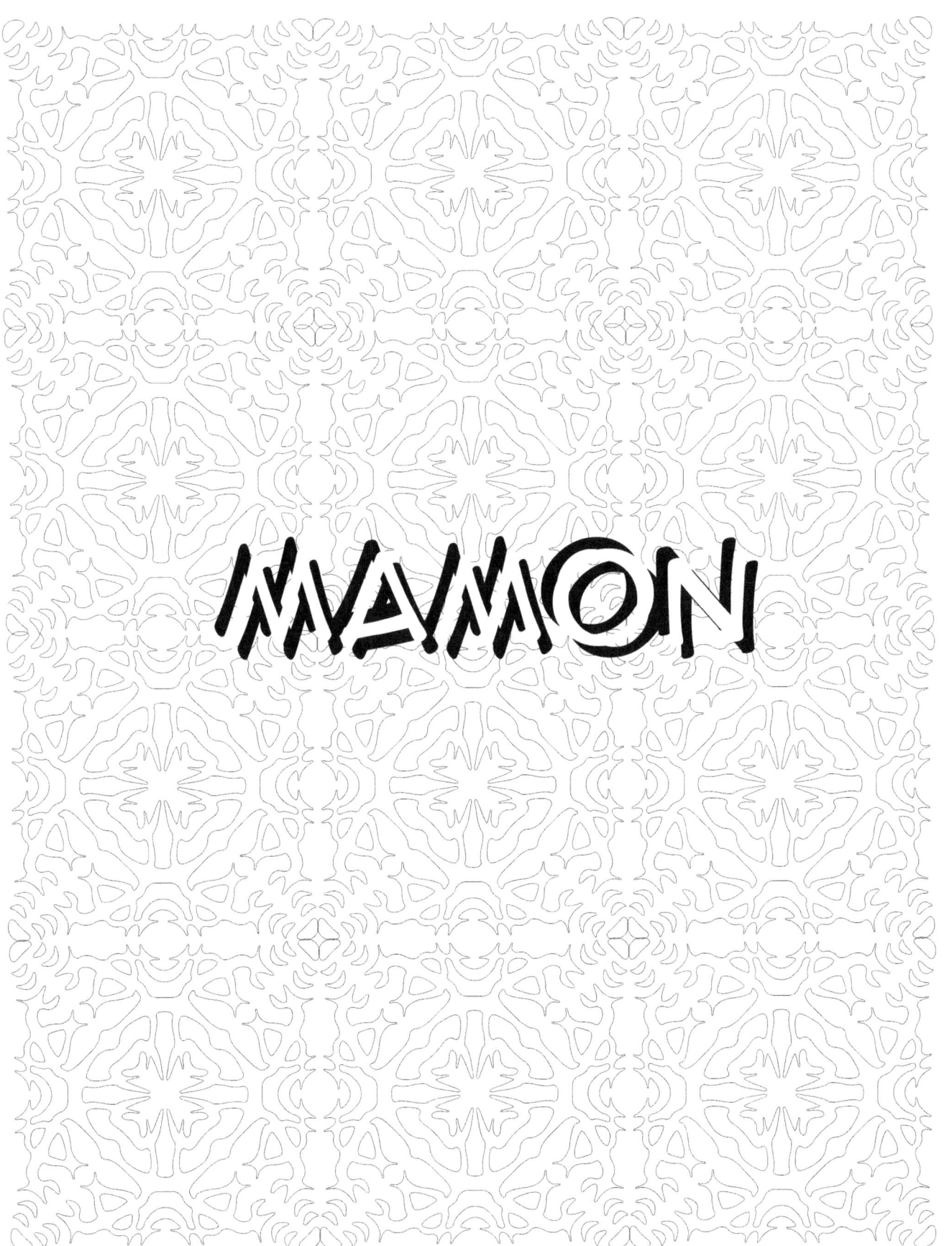

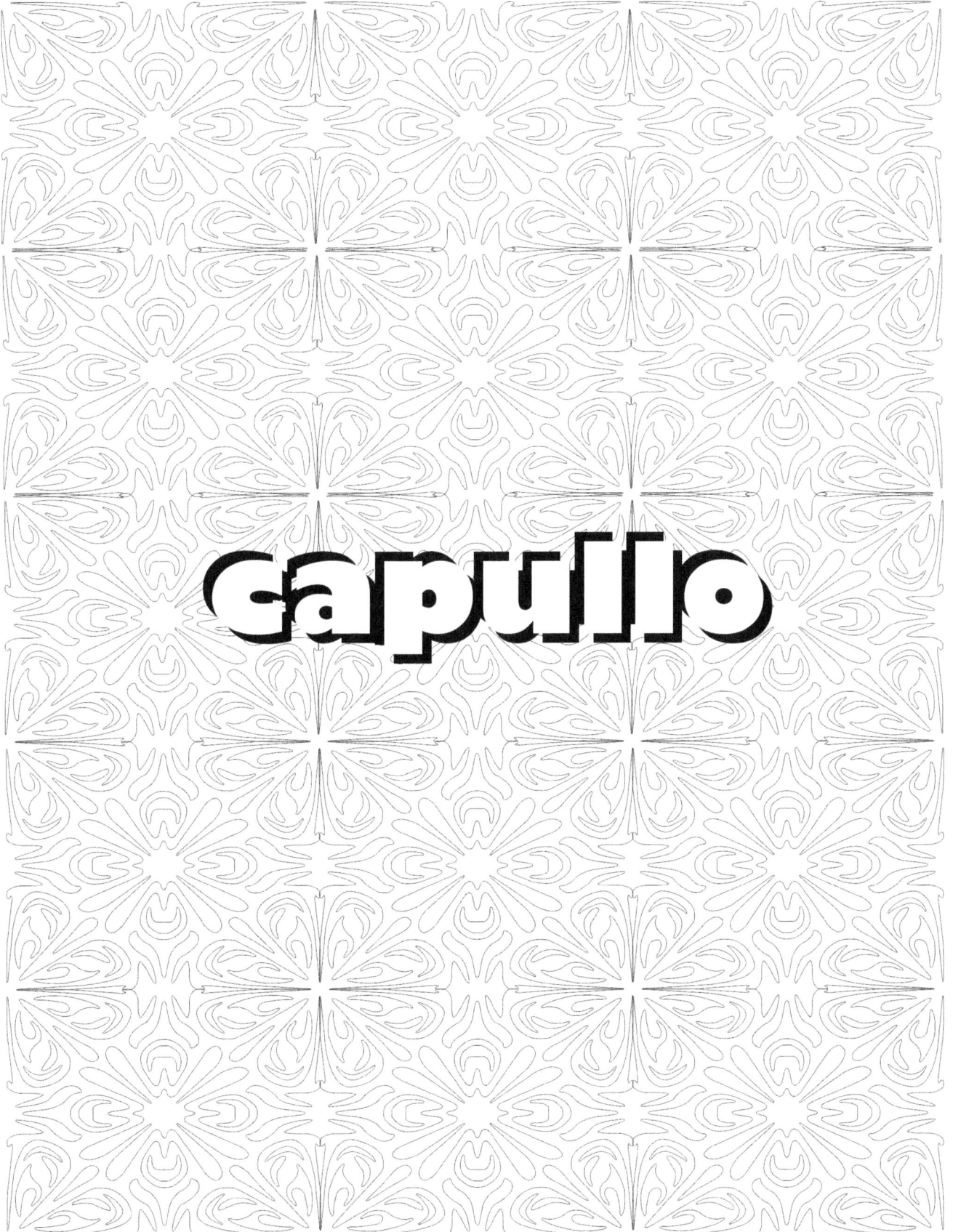

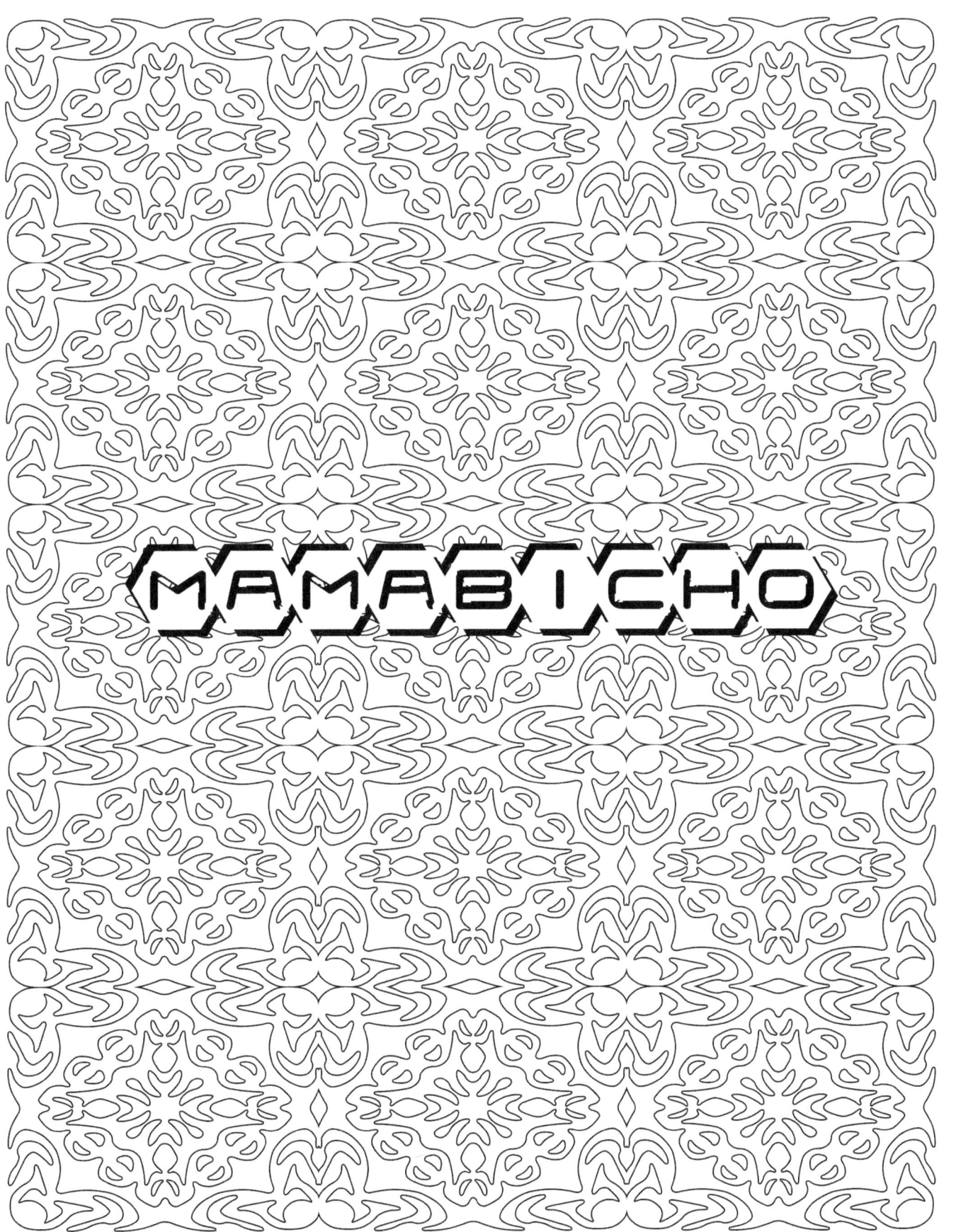

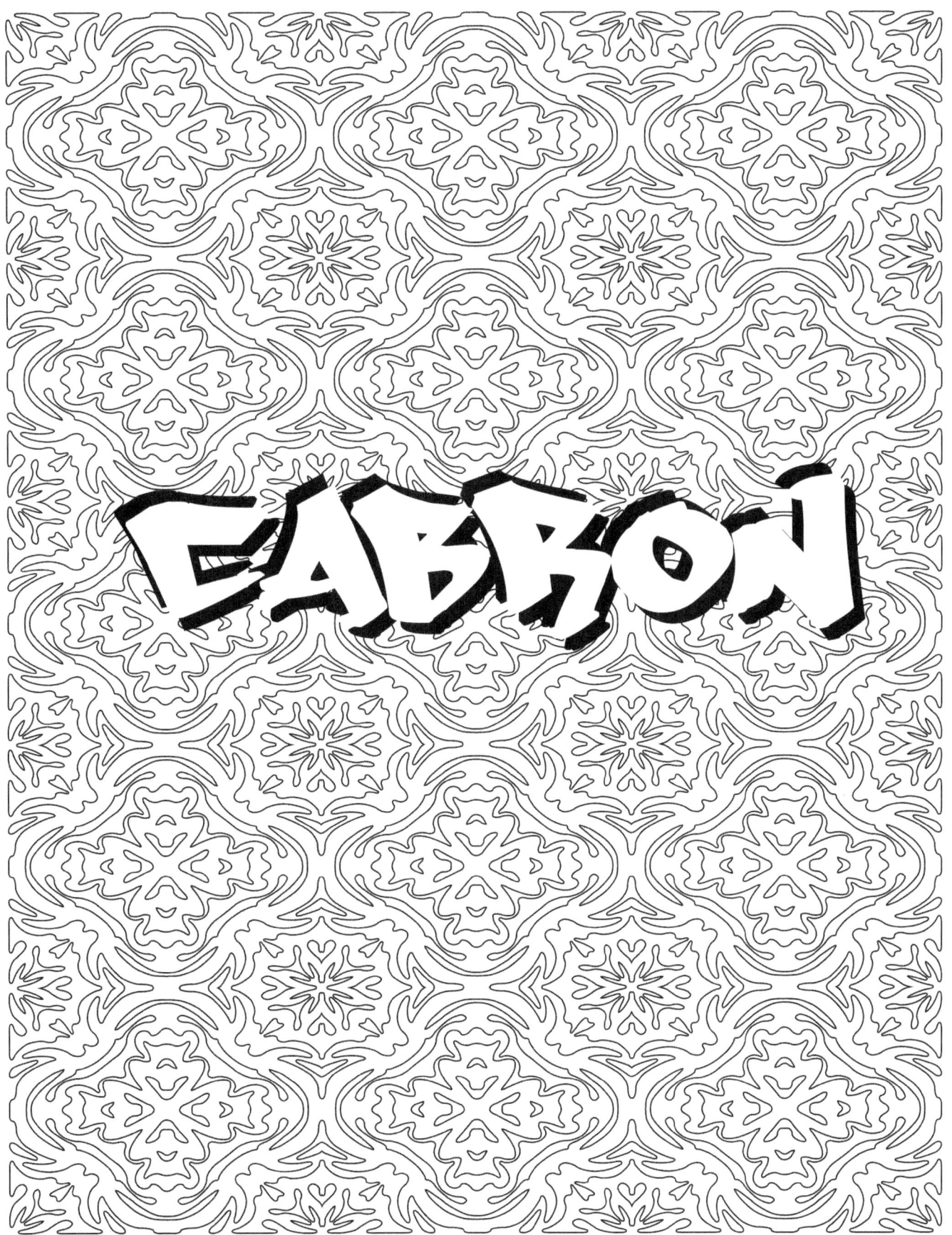

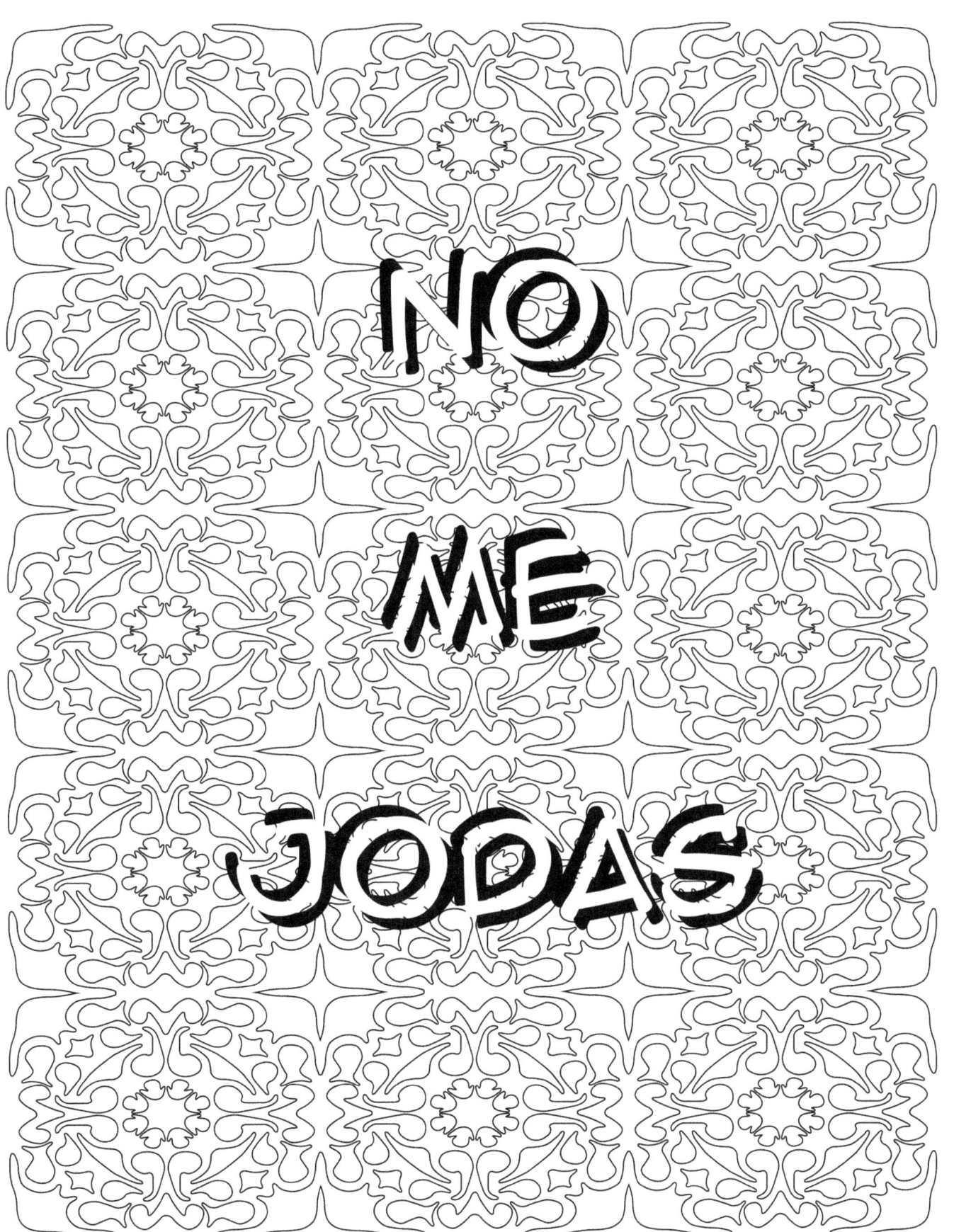

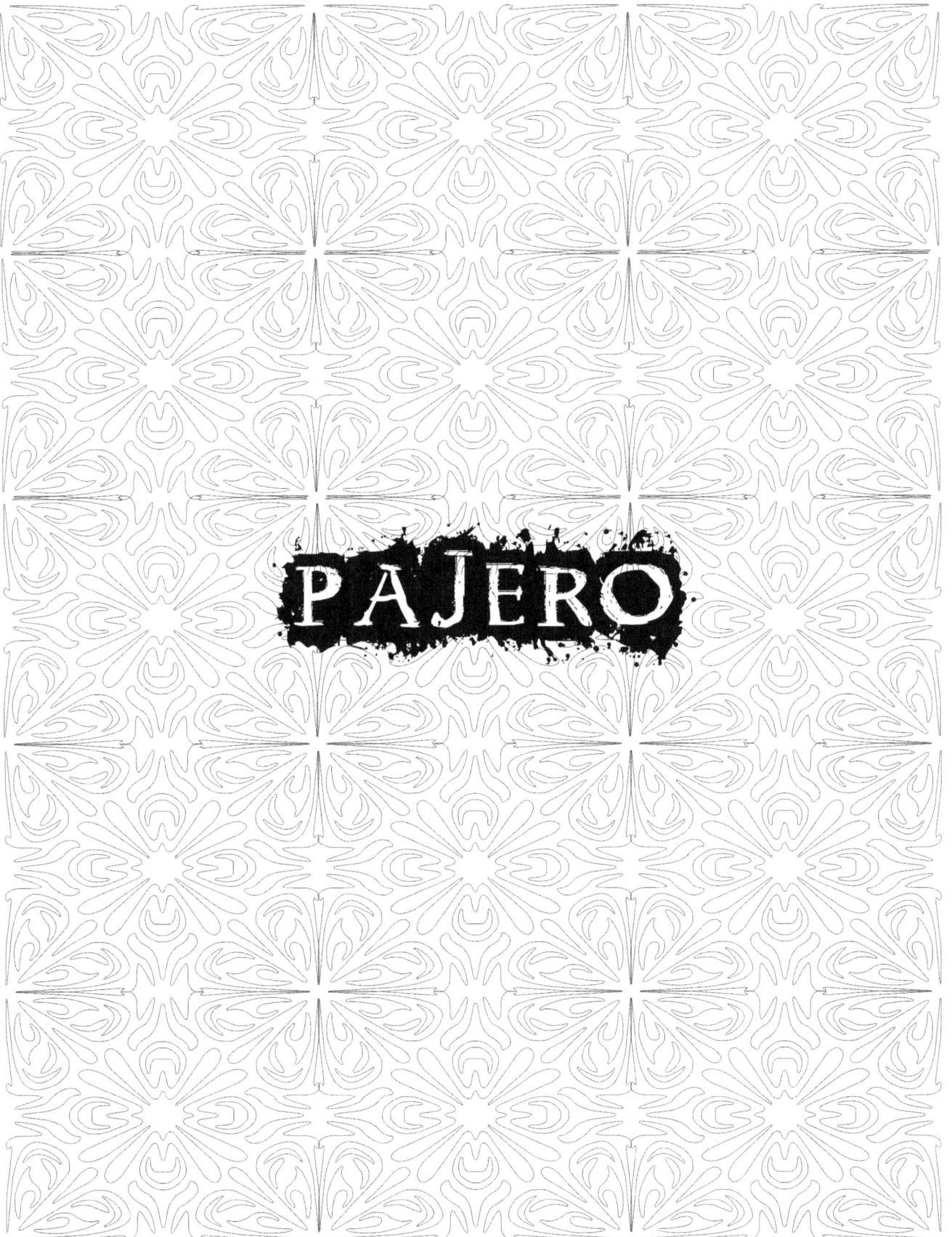

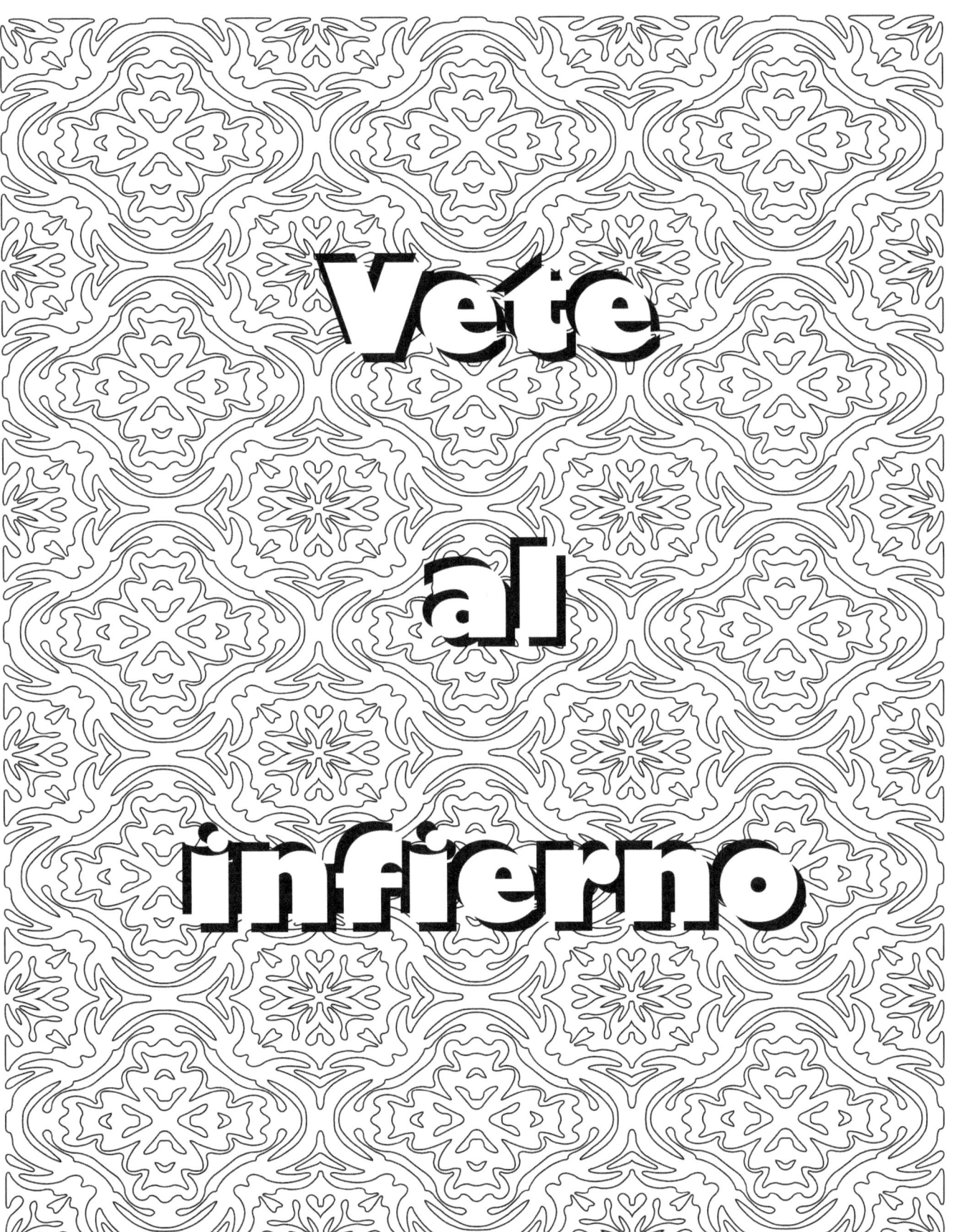

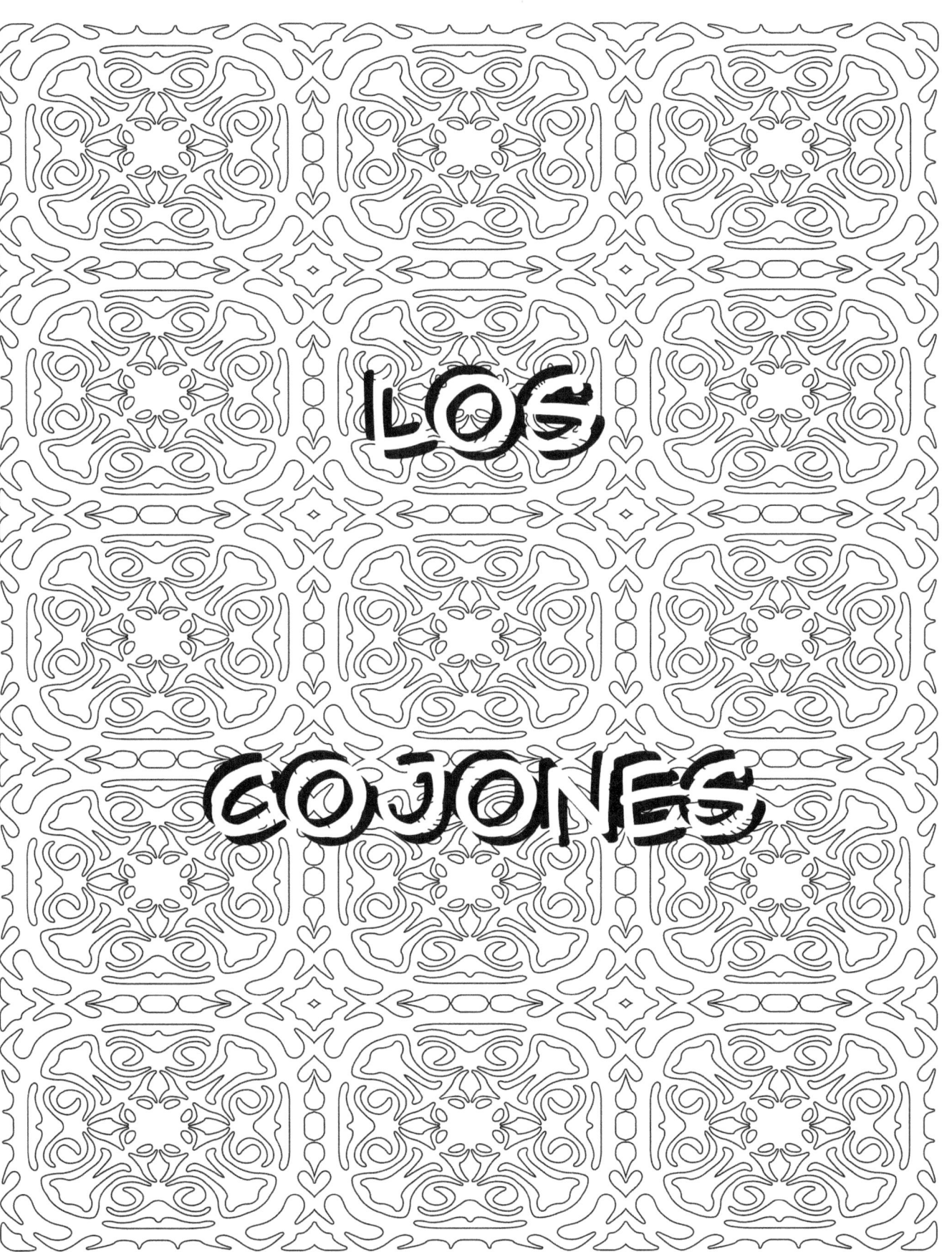

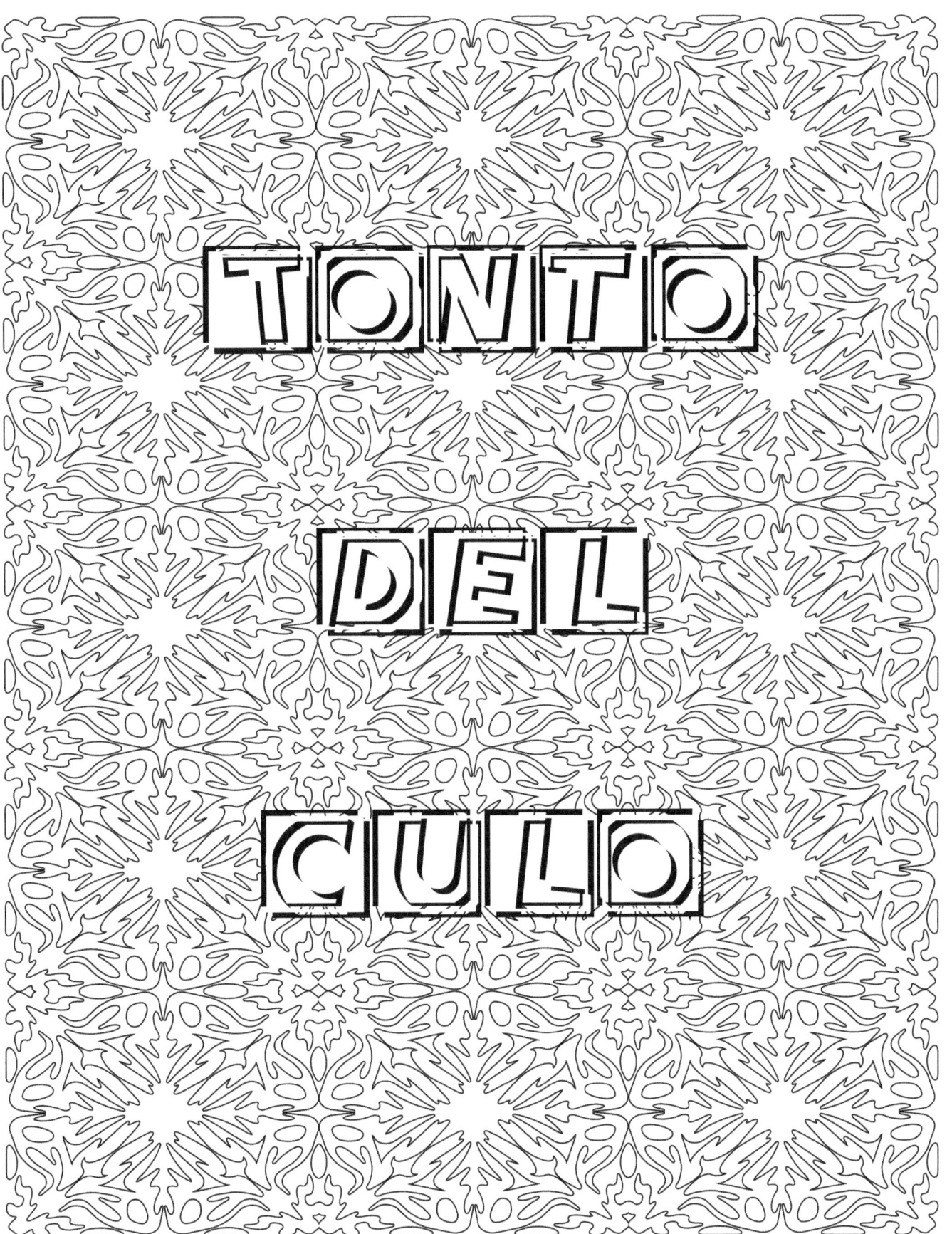

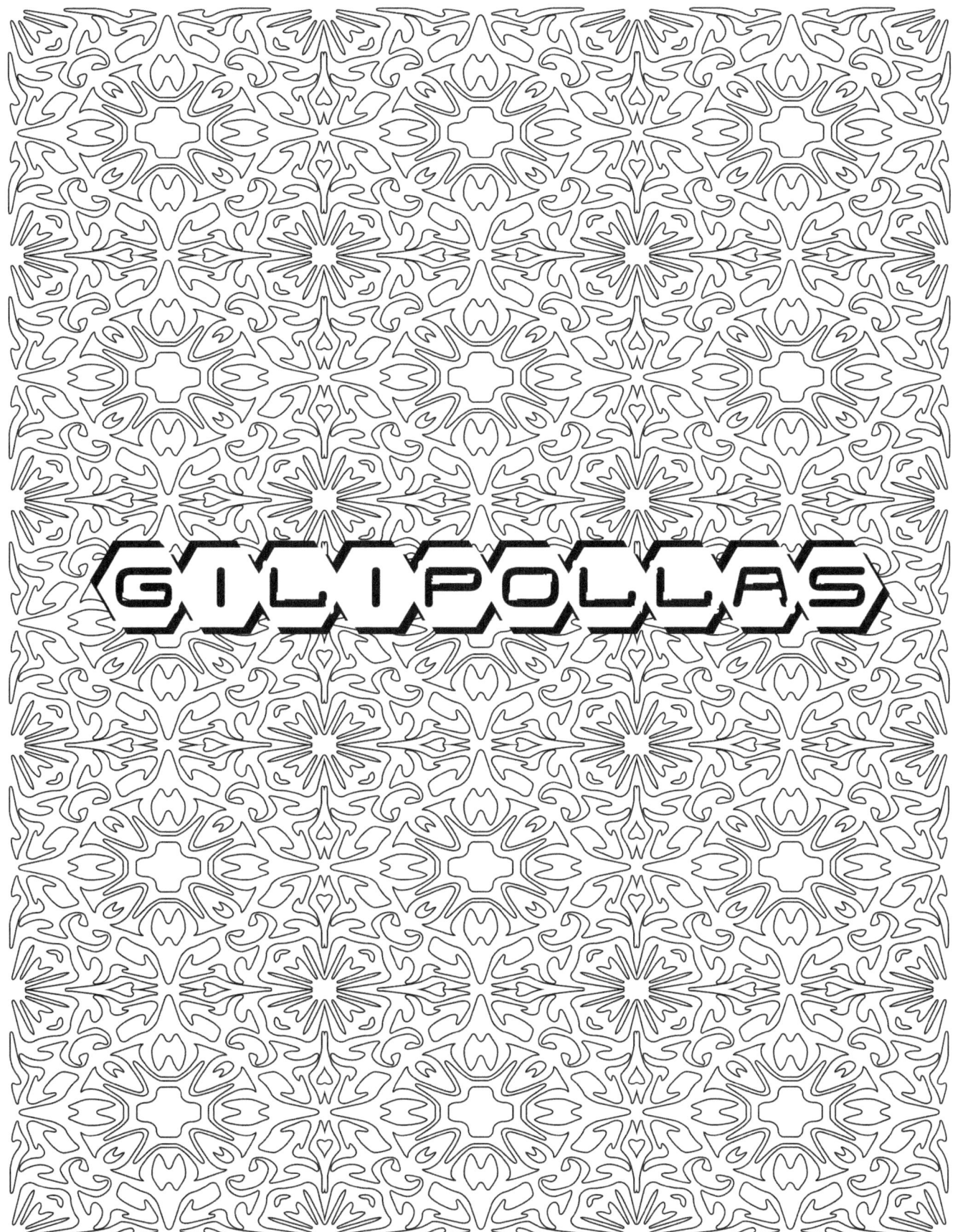

POLLAS

EN

VINAGRE

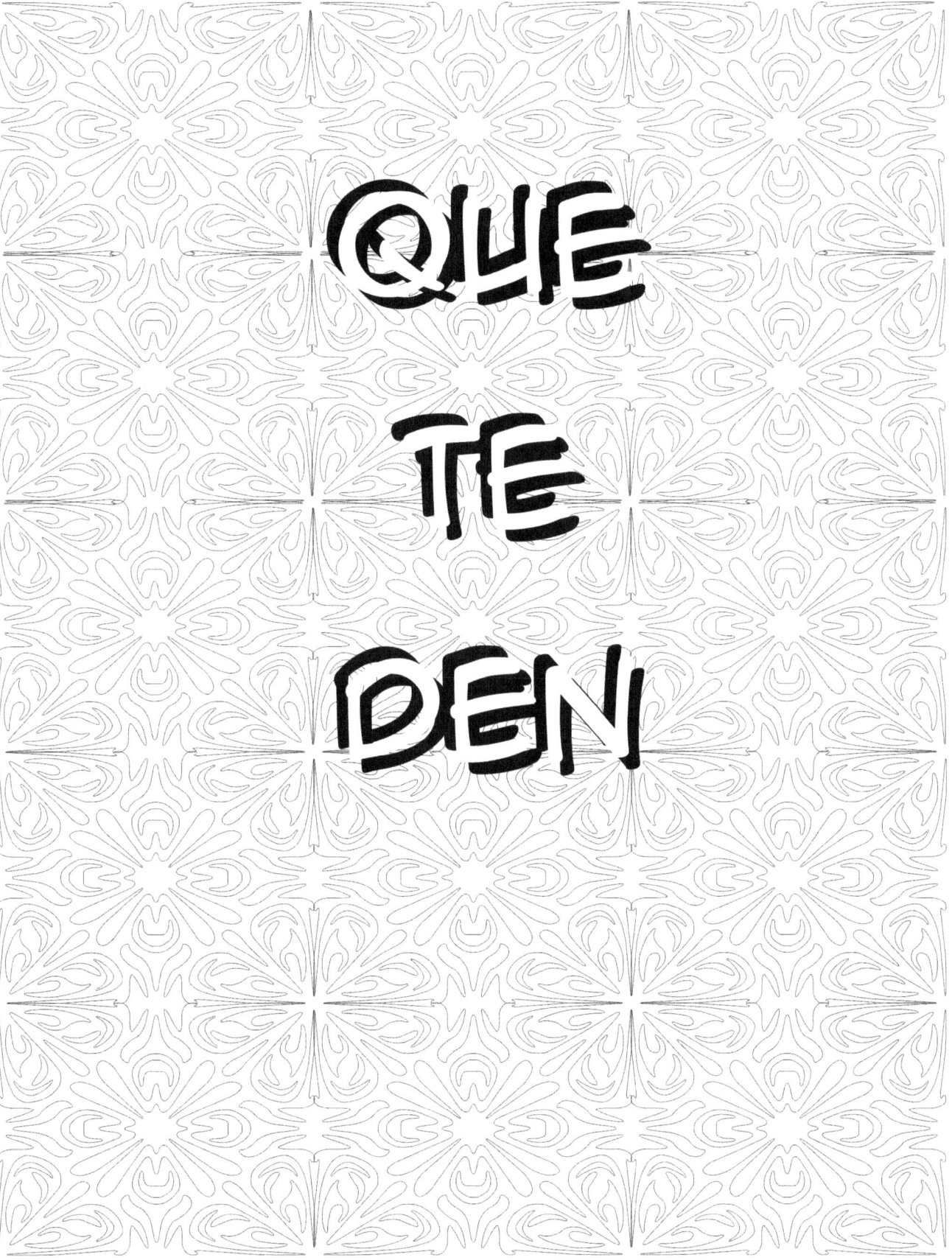

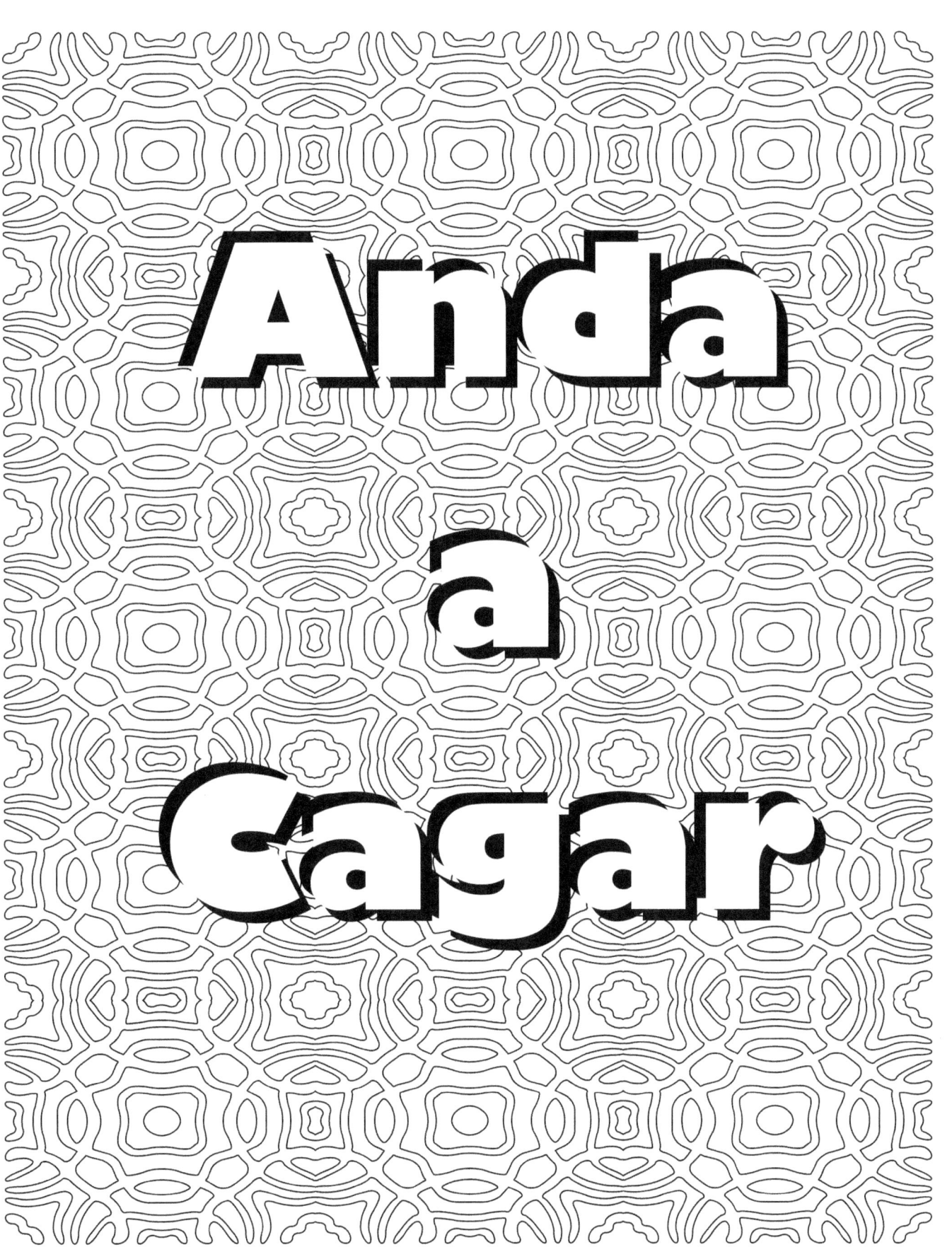

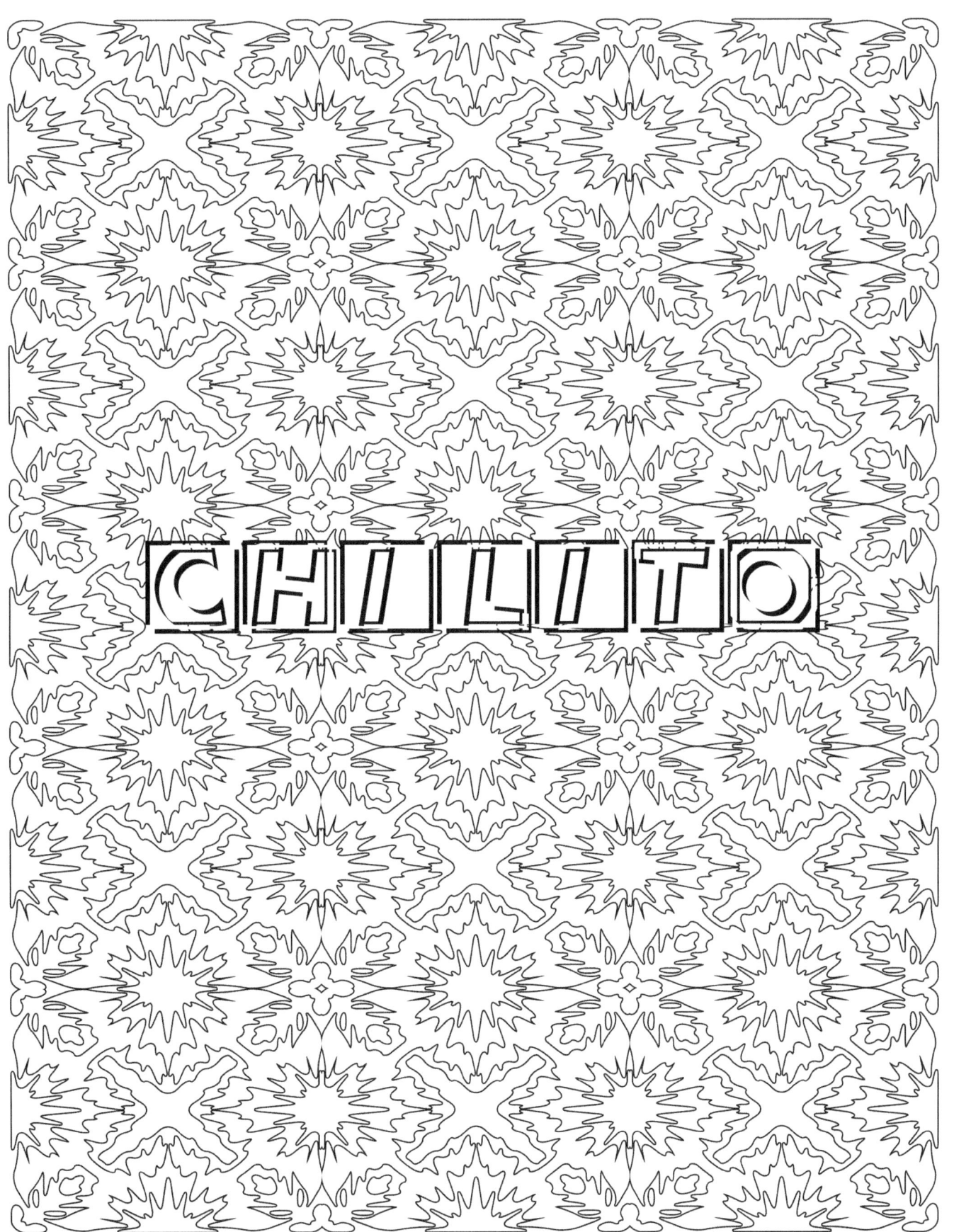

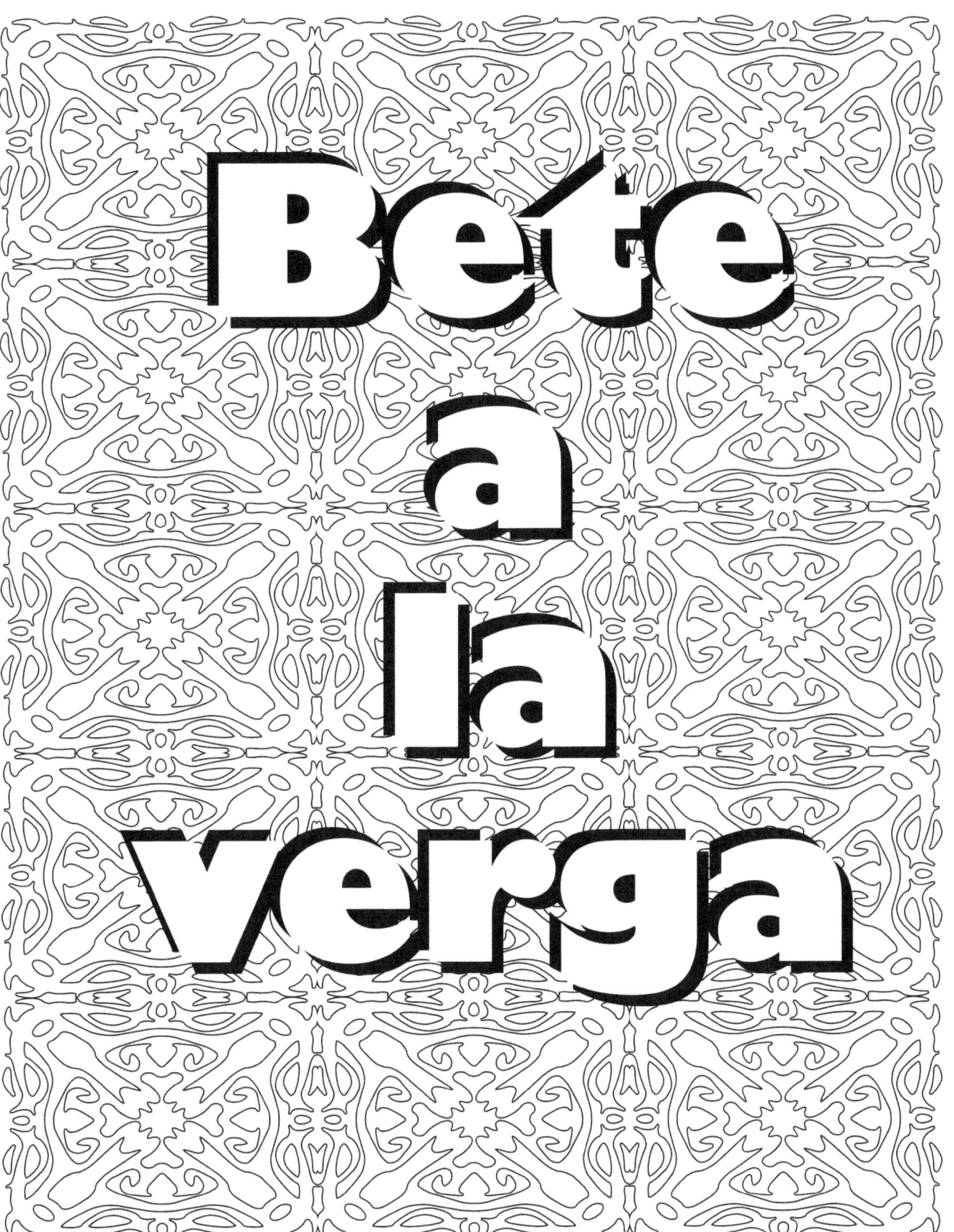

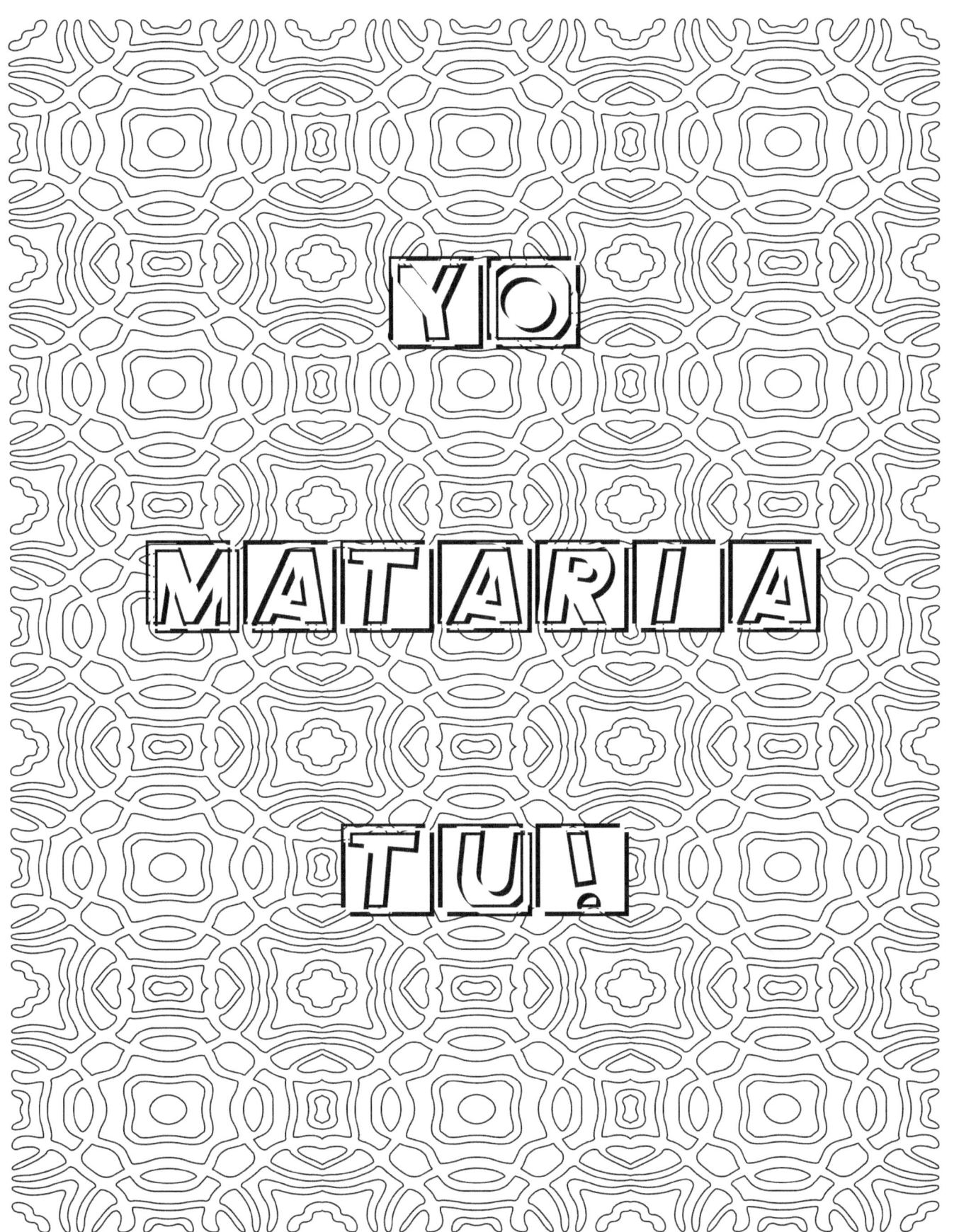

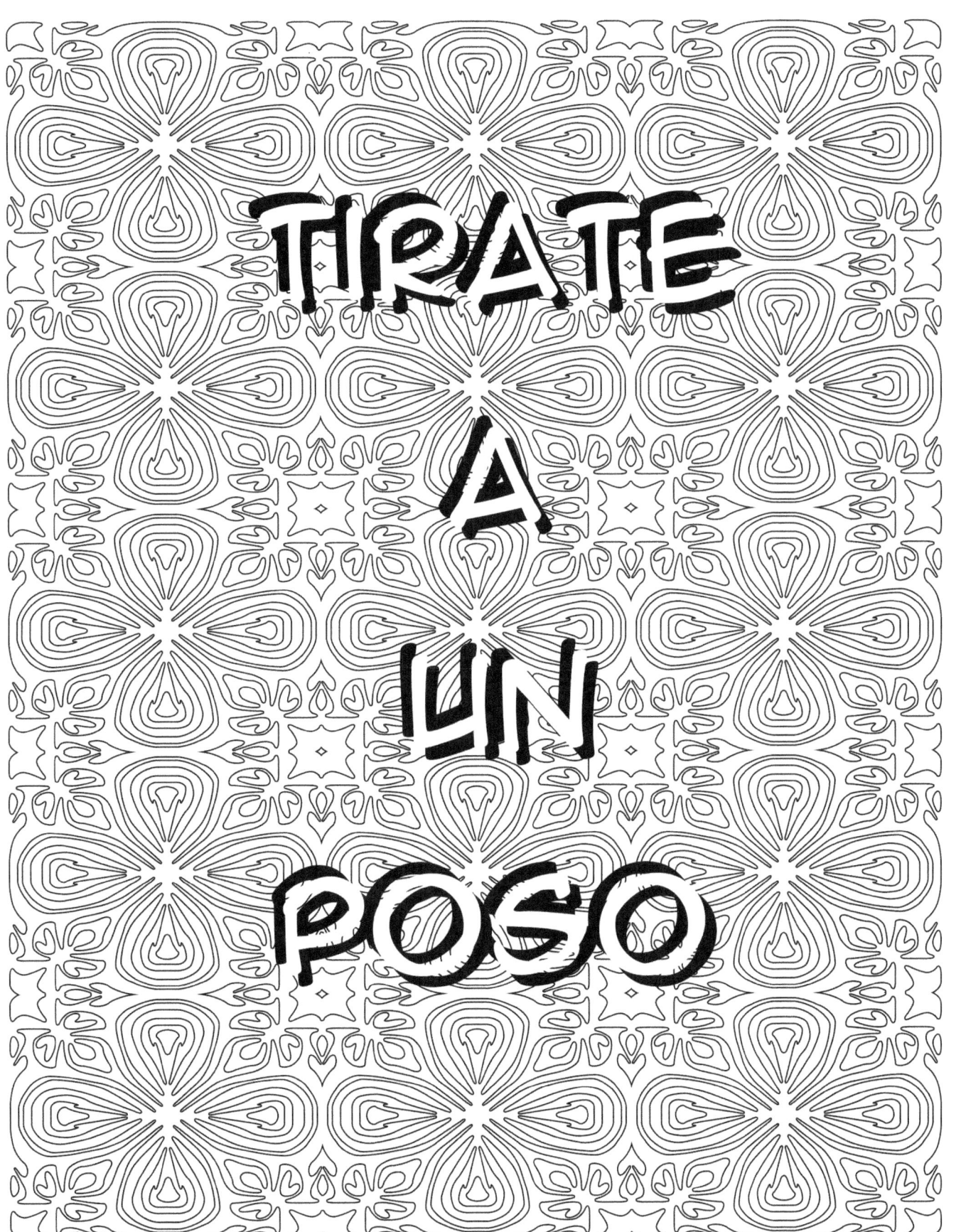

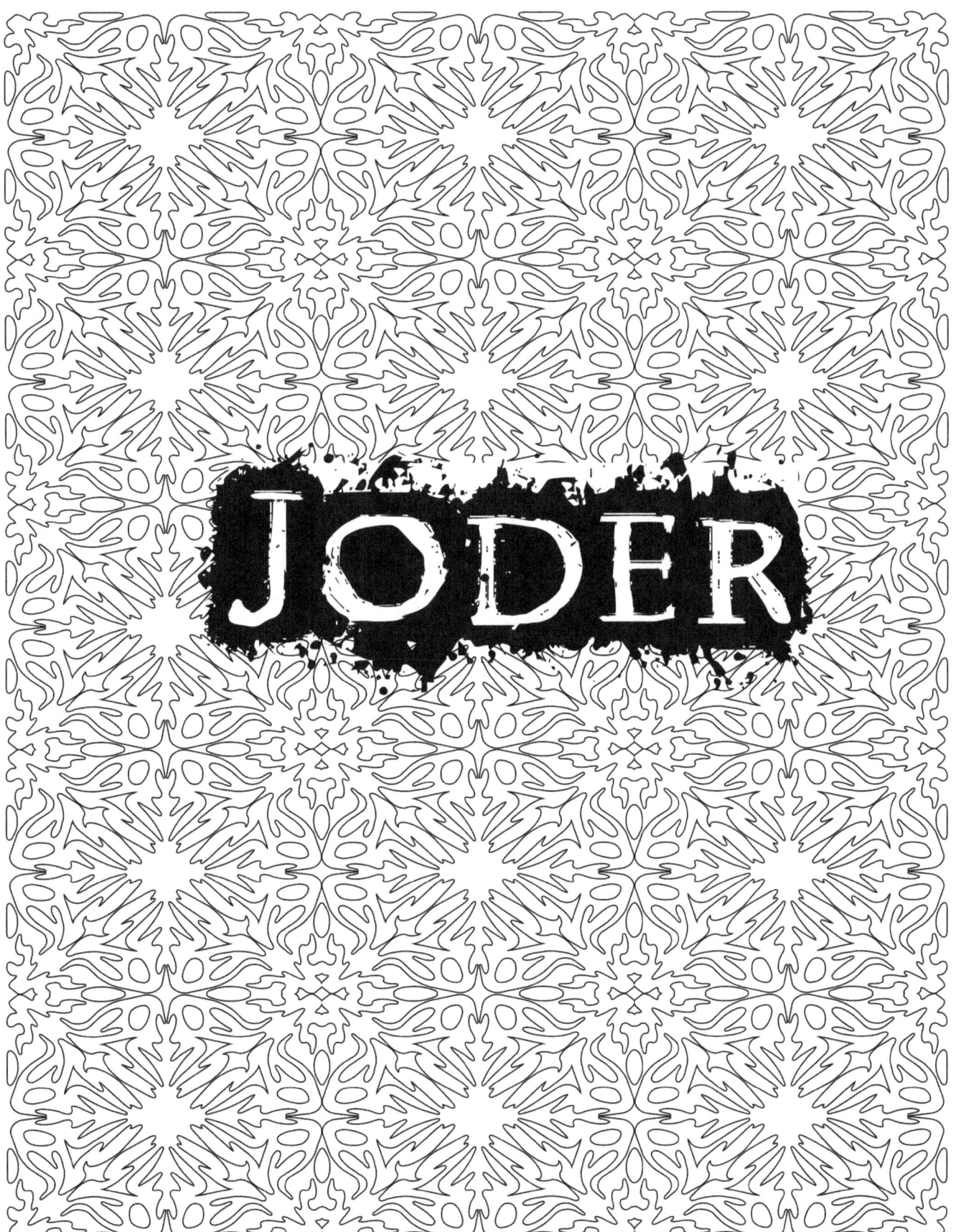

Chinga tu madre

Final Words

Now Go Out There And Start Using Those Words!

Have Fun!

www.ingramcontent.com/pod-product-compliance
Lightning Source LLC
Chambersburg PA
CBHW060002230526
45472CB00008B/1917